Happy Everything!

ON HOLD

by

Bruce Baum

On Hold

A Bruce Baum Book

Copyright 2010 by Bruce Baum

All rights reserved

ISBN   1453662677

EAN-13   9781453662670.

Front and back cover by Susan Leonard Kincade.

First Edition

Other books by Bruce Baum

Letters From A Nut   co-authored as Ted L. Nancy

More Letters From   co-authored as Ted L. Nancy

Extra Nutty   co-authored as Ted L. Nancy
(Even More Letters From A Nut)

Coming Soon:

The Adventures of Babyman comic book!

For an autographed copy of **On Hold** or, if available,
any of the first three **Letters From A Nut books** -- or
any other Bruce Baum info and stuff, please visit:
BruceBaum.com

On Hold can also be found at **Amazon.com,
BarnesandNoble.com** and a host of other e-places.

Feel free to e-mail Bruce at   **Bruce@BruceBaum.com**

Dedication

This book is dedicated to my parents, Leonard and Marilyn Baum, who made sure there was always laughter in the house. Also, my funny wife Lynn, my funny kids Jenna and Dylan, and my funny brother and sister, Marla and Stuart.

Thanks

I would also like to shout out a special thanks to John and Sue Kincade, Mark, Aaron and Leah Saltzman, Jim McPartland, and Brian Tiffany. They're all funny too.

TABLE OF CONTENTS

(cont'd)

TABLE OF CONTENTS

EXPLANATION

EXPLANATION

When you call someone or some place and they put you "on hold," they control you. Maybe it's because I was raised in "the land of the free" that this irks everything irkable in me.

Would you allow a clerk in a store to grab you by the ears as soon as you walked in and hold you in place until they were ready to talk to you? While they talked to someone else? I think not! At the very least, that might be temporary involuntary imprisonment, or some kind of mild kidnapping. In some states, I think you could almost go to jail for that. Why then, do we allow, indeed, make it legal, on the phone?

I demand control of my ears! What's next, my nose? Should I refuse to patronize the people and businesses that "on hold" me? Great. No cable, no phones, no utilities, no credit, no friends. But I certainly can't continue yelling at innocent furniture when I'm "on hold." It's bad for me. And it can't be good for my furniture.

In an effort to turn my aggravating conundrum into something possibly positive, I conducted, and funded with loose change, an independent experimental stress-release study. When I was put "on hold," I would write. Whatever came to mind. Just let my head roam range-free. Short stories that I might come back to, quick thoughts, poems, blurps, ideas, frustrations -- whatever popped into my head was in-bounds. My phone and my computer would become my laboratory. My pants would remain my pants.

Therefore, this book is a diary, if you will, of my time spent "on hold" during Phase One of my amateur mental-health experiment, designed to turn frustrating hostility into an unfettered, rumpled voice .

THE FIRST ONES

Who Needs A Conductor?

What's up with the conductor? Hey, I like to go to the symphony as much as the next guy. Especially when the next guy doesn't like to go.
But a conductor? You either know the song or you don't. I assume most of these guys have been playing their instruments for awhile. Learn the song. C'mon, you already have the sheet music in front of you. As long as you all start together, what's the problem? I mean, I can understand if you're just learning how to play -- maybe then you need a conductor and a cheat-sheet. Are they too lazy to learn the song? Can't keep a beat?
Poor memories? If you don't have rhythm and you can't learn a song, then start a jazz band. No one will know. You don't see U-2 or Aerosmith using a conductor and charts. They learn the song. Practice together a few times if you need to. Tell the guys, "You blow hard here, you drum softly there," and you go do the show. Who is going to know if you screw up?
If anyone complains, you tell them: "Hey, that was <u>our</u> rendition."
It's worked for Joe Cocker and UB-40.

And if you are going to have a conductor, how about some entertainment? Look at any band major. Talk about multi-tasking. He's marching around, twirling a baton, throwing it in the air, catching it, cartwheeling, spinning, bouncing, bending, doing neat hat tricks, the splits, juggling, AND conducting. This guy puts on a show AND conducts a MOVING orchestra. He brings something to the table. The conductor stands there waving a skinny stick. At anchored musicians. What if I don't like the song? At least give me something to watch. Hey Mr. Conductor Man, give me a show or buy a ticket and watch with the rest of us.

One more thing:

How Come?

Nobody writes symphonies anymore. How come? There was a time when they were all the rage. Oh sure, a few guys still do, but not like they all did during The Renaissance. Back then, most of the popular musical pieces were symphonies. Once in awhile a concerto or naughty limerick might cross-over. In fact , the bawdiest limerick to enter the charts during The Renaissance was "In Da Pub" by Fitty-Pence. The lyrics were never allowed to be printed, only heard.

So what happened to the symphony? Plus, with symphonies you get more bang for your buck. Imagine how long a lap dance lasted back then. The short, unfinished symphonies were thirty minutes. Nowadays, you pay twenty dollars and you get a two-minute tantric shuffle. If you're lucky. Back then, for a farthing, you got a half-hour of squirming damsel on your equator. Some places even allowed mutual writhing. And I'll tell you something, that's what this country needs: a good twenty-dollar lap dance with an overture.

HERE'S THE SITUATION:
YOU'RE IN THE VATICAN IN A PICKUP GAME OF BASKETBALL AND YOU'RE ONE OF THE CAPTAINS CHOOSING SIDES. DO YOU HAVE TO PICK THE POPE FIRST IF THERE'S A BETTER PLAYER AVAILABLE? I'M NOT SAYING THERE IS, BUT, THEOLOGICALLY, WHAT IF? I WOULD THINK THE POPE WOULD WANT TO BE PICKED FAIR AND SQUARE, NO FAVORS. C'MON, THE POPE DOES HIS TALKING ON THE COURT. AND I THINK IT'S RIGHTEOUS HOW HE'S ALWAYS WORKING ON HIS GAME -- THE LAST TO LEAVE THE GYM. EVEN AFTER THE GAME OR A PRACTICE, HE'S SHOOTING FREE THROWS, CROSS-DRIBBLING BEHIND HIS BACK, OR BREAKING IN A NEW SHOT. ANOTHER THING: IN SOFTBALL, NEVER INTENTIONALLY WALK SOMEONE TO GET TO THE POPE. HE HATES THAT. (AND "YOU-KNOW-WHO'" HATES IT EVEN MORE.) THE ODDS ARE AGAINST YOU ANYWAY. HE HITS .993 UNDER THOSE CONDITIONS. YOU PITCH TO THE POPE AND YOU TAKE YOUR LUMPS.

What happens when two charities collide? Suppose the Make a Wish Foundation receives a request from a terminally ill someone, explaining that their lifelong wish was to spank a penguin. How would Greenpeace and Friends of the Earth react? Would the charities become contentious and sap each other's resources, attempting to implement their own agenda? Or, will they agree to let things slide just this once, and try to find a tough penguin? Preferrably with a fetish. Let us hope it never happens. But let us be prepared if it does.

***

What came first -- the salami or the bologna? Whichever one came first, some-one must have said: "Hey! I can make a better meat log than that." Also, there's a lot more different salamis than bolognas. You got salami, dried salami, italian salami, kosher salami -- the list goes on. Salami diversified. Bologna is bologna . Oh sure, you can put some pimentos and olives and pepper in bologna. But that just turns it into "lunchmeat." It's not even bologna any more. You can do a bunch of stuff to salami and it's still a salami. Bologna probably came first because it's so easy to beat. If salami came first, no one would have even tried to make bologna. You know what? It doesn't matter which one came first. Salami is better.

EXTREME LISTENING

I'm really into X-treme Listening. Sometimes I listen to the same thing over and over and over for eight days. Or quickly for an hour. Sometimes I'll listen to something just once, but I listen really hard. I've listened to things in outer space through a microphone on a rocket.

I've listened to a bug inside my ear for its' complete life-cycle.
I've listened to what other people were listening to, and wondered
if they would have heard it better if I wasn't listening so hard. I've heard stuff
no one else was listening to, and I've listened to stuff no one else wanted to hear.

Once, I thought I heard nothing, but it turned out to be me listening very softly
from a distance.

*****

Even though he knows it could affect the balance of our ecosystem,
Larrimer continues to breed and release black-widow spiders that love to
cuddle after mating.

Manjo Manjo

"Manjo Manjo," the oldest known song with lyrics, was sung by several closely-knit primitive tribes. It went something like this:

Manjo manjo manjo manjo
Manjo manjo manjo lu.

Many musical anthropologists suggest that "Manjo Manjo" is the first song to express an idea with a beginning, a middle, and an end. No one is sure what the word "manjo" means, but they know "lu" means "that's my nose."

*****

Scenario:
You are blind, have numb fingertips, can't smell, and the person that you marry, unbeknownst to you, has "multiple-personality disorder." Now, the first time your new spouse changes their personality, you are oblivious due to your sensory deprivation, and you have what you think is an affair with someone you think is a stranger. But it's not. It's actually your legitimate spouse.
Is that cheating because you thought it was? Or is it a "no-harm, no foul" situation based on the presumption that "reality" trumps perception and intent?

THE MAN WHO CAUGHT FISH WITH A SPOON

Larrimer, the man, waded into the icy waters of the American River. He bent over so his lips barely cleared the cold, flowing current, dipped his ladle into the water, and holding it very still, began to hum, tweet and belch. Mesmerized, fish would snuggle into the large spoon's basin. Sometimes, I swear, you could hear the fish purr. If I didn't know better, I'd say they were flirting with Larrimer. What was it about Larrimer's blurtles? Were the fish hypnotized? No matter, Larrimer slowly lifted the spoon from the crisp stream. The fish would lay still and trusting. And though now literally a fish out of water, a calm contentment washed over it. That is, until Larrimer slapped it onto a hot grill. Then, the fish got real mad, real fast, and used the "F" word. A lot.

HEY PHONE COMPANY! ACT LIKE ONE.

HEY PHONE COMPANY! ACT LIKE ONE.

I've been "on hold" with my wireless phone company for twenty minutes. For the fifth time today. That's a hundred minutes! So far. How stupid is that? The phone company hasn't hired enough people to answer their phones. They're a phone company. How do you misjudge that? Phone stuff should be your specialty. Expect lots of calls. Hire lots of people so the rest of the world doesn't have to slow down to your speed. You're the pace car. A communications epicenter has responsibilities.

Unfortunately, this is not a fluke. Regardless, I wait again at the core of all "on-holdness."

Each time I finally get to talk to a person, I explain the situation, they put me on hold to work on it, and are gone so long, that I get disconnected. After a few times, I explain to my new diplomat: "I've called and waited 20 minutes, several times, to talk to someone, and I keep getting cut off in the middle of resolving the situation. So if you put me "on hold" and we get disconnected, can you please call me back so I don't have to go over everything all over again with someone new after another twenty minute wait?"

Get this: She says, "I can't do that. We can only get incoming calls here. We can't make outgoing calls."

"Wait a minute." I'm shocked. "You work at the phone company and you can't make an outgoing call? They gave you a one-way, remedial phone? Criminey Pete! Alexander Graham Bell had a better hookup. Everyone else in the world has a two-way phone that takes pictures, video, text messages, internets, shaves, prints, copies, downloads, tases, finds fish, beams tanning rays, repels insects, gives directions, edits, projects, records, and analyzes particles. And they get them from your company!"

I can't stop and blab on:

"The phone company gave you a beginners phone. Heck, it's not even a phone! It's closer to a walkie-talkie. Actually, it's just a 'walkie.' Or a 'talkie.' But it's certainly not both. No outgoing calls? You have to be shittin' me. That's dangerous," I warned. "What would happen if a madman burst into your office and taped dry ice to your thighs? Or to your cheeks. What if he taped your thighs to your cheeks. Or made them stick together with the dry ice. You wouldn't even see what was going on. Or what if you got a nice piece of fish lodged in your throat? Or your hair caught fire? You can't call out for help."

(cont'd)

"You work for the company that sells state-of-the-art communication devices to the world -- in some instances, they give them away -- and you can't make an outgoing phone-call to save your freezing thighs or your flaming head. From THEIR office.

The phone company gave you the shittiest phone they have. Actually, by definition, if you can't call out, it's not even a real fuckin' phone. What the hell did you do, that they don't trust you with a real phone?"

To all that she replies: "Please don't swear, sir."

"Please don't swear?" I question. "Fuck fuck fuck. Shitty shitty fuck fuck. Who you gonna call?"

THE NEXT CHAPTER

PICKLEFUDGE

Vic made the best pickle-fudge anyone had ever tasted. Some say he made the only pickle-fudge anyone had ever tasted. Regardless, it tasted wonderful. Vic's land produced cucumber pickles that were so tasty, they were fudge-able. The karma that flowed through the Earth at that particular spot must have been very unique. The air was different there, too. You could taste it. Many believed Vic himself was one of the ingredients -- that his land and the things that grew on it reacted to him as if he was the secret sauce in a prize-winning recipe -- the last piece of a unique agri-culinary jigsaw puzzle. Plants grew for him. Some folks said you could almost see the trees smile when he came around. Those folks were loaded onto a flat-bed truck, then tagged, and released in another town. Legend has it that the insects policed themselves, and that the harmful ones had agreed to a no-fly zone over Vic's fields. The crops were always happiest when Vic was around. And how the cucumbers loved him. Perhaps they knew what the future held and looked forward to being fudged.

SOME HISTORY

History tells us that Anne Boleyn had three breasts, and six fingers on each hand. That almost made her and the king a threesome. In theory, she could simultaneously satisfy the king, herself, and play the lute. Today, worst-case scenario, she's in Las Vegas starring in Crazy Girls.

What if historians actually meant Anne Boleyn had three breasts and six fingers ON EACH of her hands. (Eight breasts, twelve fingers overall) Perhaps Dickens left us a hint when he wrote of "being slapped silly by the odd hand of Anne Boleyn."

*****

Some planets don't keep time. No clocks. No watches.
They just say "see you later," and you know by how loud they say it, when that will be.

You Can't Hide Your Driving Eyes

When approaching a highway speed limit sign, where does the speed limit start ? Is it where the speed limit sign *is*, or does it start when you *see* the speed limit sign? I think it's when you see it. You may argue that people with better eyesight get to go faster sooner. Aha! But they also have to slow down sooner. A true yin and yang. Or yang and yin, depending on which direction you're traveling.

*****

I was in an elevator with Chuck Mangione and I thought he said, "The man who can make music with his nose, needs not a flugelhorn. I am not that man." My wife said he clearly mumbled, "Hey there."

THE WOMMAN WITH THE FOXXY BELLY

Pot-bellies are attractive on very few people. You've got Chris Farley,
Benjamin Franklin, Jackie Gleason, and maybe the guys in Bachman
Turner   Overdrive. But Tillie was different. She was the only woman I had
ever laid eyes on that looked absolutely ravishing with a big belly. To
paraphrase Rod Stewart: "She wore it well." You couldn't imagine her
any other way. And it made you wonder why more women couldn't pull
off the paunch thing. Her tummy was full of sass. It was supple, yet more
dangerous than a boxer's wallop. More than one boisterous goon found
that out. Hers was an erotically bulbous, forbidden abdomen. You longed
to ride on it. Or maybe rest your head on its' crest. But you knew you
never would. Perhaps that was its' allure.

I recently peeked out the kitchen window and saw a raccoon humping my cat, while my cat paw-banged a bird. I asked a zoologist if that was normal, and he told me, "No. That would be like you fucking a bear while the bear gave some lizard a hand job."

That's not normal either?

*****

I believe The Bible says: "an eye for an eye, and a tooth for a tooth."
But what if you get beat up by a blind, toothless guy?
Can you just rip off one of his cheeks and call it even?

HOW COME ? #17

Except in cartoons, long-necked birds never look back over
their shoulders when they fly. How come? I'll tell you.
Let's say a duck is flying fast, against the wind. If the duck
looks backward to check things out --- ZZZZZIP -- the wind
pins the bird's head to it's side, so the duck can only look
behind itself, giving it no idea where it is headed. The fear
of flying neck-first into a tree or mountain causes the duck to
flap harder and faster in an effort to right itself, causing it to fly
in circles -- becoming a spinning duck-ring in the sky -- until it
collapses from exhaustion and hopefully rights itself during
freefall before it hits the ground. Usually, when you see a
bird stumbling around like it's drunk, that's what happened.

MOONLIGHTING

I am training pit bulls to attack rear-first. That way, no one gets hurt. They still bark, and growl, and snort, but they strike with their tushy. It's very scary.
In fact, most people think: "if that dog thinks he can whip me with just his ass, I'm out of here."

Those that stand their ground, encounter a relentless, blitzing booty, intent on humiliating them into submission, implanted between their tight, muscular butt-cheeks and then shaken like a ragdoll. Life threatening? Not really.
A demeaning deterrent? Indeed.

****

Recently, I found a little corner of the world that's round. It is the exception to every rule of physics, engineering, and thumb. It is a very secret place, so all I am allowed to say is: It's no where near Macon, Georgia. So don't look there.

Hermits Unite!

Hermit-Fest is on! I've got one guy coming, so we're sold out. Act now and sign up for next year! Before someone else does.

Larry and Joan both had multiple personalities. Ironically, all of their personalities dated each other, and together the two of them raised a number of different families. Their offspring inherited the same syndrome. So my question is this: How does the census bureau handle that ? Perhaps more important, but perhaps not, is what would a philosopher think? Is each personality its' own 'zone'? Its' own person? Can more than one "being" inhabit one physical entity? And if so, are they entitled to read each other's mail?

Larrimer trained his dogs to rob vending machines. He was often foiled by the trail of change that led to his back door.

I once saw a male magistrate dressed incognito as a female prostitute. And I was prepared to make a citizen's arrest, when I realized, you can't book a judge by his cover.

I just bought a beautiful Hawaiin shirt, made from hemp, for three bucks a gram.

I once saw a 1-0 ballgame that was so close, the side that had 1 kept changing.

MORE HISTORY

Before he became known as "The Hun," Attila was lauded for a plethora of jobs well done. In his early teens, he was Attila The Clown, gigging at fairs, sacrifices, inter-fiefdom competitions, and food orgies. Later, his hand-eye coordination in a soccer-like game became legendary, and fans cheered him as Attila the Goalie. When he meticulously ran the empire's bath houses he was addressed as Attila The Attendant. But it wasn't until he released, then suppressed, then harnessed, then suppressed a little, and then unleashed the powerful traits of all three, that he became the ruthless leader of the notoriously feared, pillaging Hunnies.

*****

There will come a time in the future when we've been around so long,
The Middle Ages can't be called the The Middle Ages anymore, and it
will have to be called The Last Part of The Beginning Ages.

Depending on when you are reading this, it may have already happened.

THOUGHTS ON SPACE PERUSAL

According to what I think I have been taught, each cell of our body contains the DNA codes that allow us to follow our ancestry back to the beginning of life. Or something like that. So, along those lines of reasoning, I suggest that each piece of space has within it a similar capacity, holding within it the events that have taken place within that space throughout time, in a cosmic file cabinet -- a storage unit of the past -- waiting to be found and screened.

Furthermore, by constructing a time-adjustable viewing space, we could literally peruse history. Not change it, but watch. Mysteries of the past could be solved. We could witness the building of The Great Pyramids and Stonehedge, behold the miracles from the Bibles, watch Lincoln at Gettysburg, Marco Polo, Cher, Sun Tzu, as well as learn the secrets of "the sliding-knot-on-the-rope trick."

Then again, if someone could tap into a space where <u>you yourself</u> had been, after you'd been there, and watch what were previouly confidential and/or intimate moments, privacy as we know it would be gone. Ironic. Privacy guaranteed only for the moment, because anyone in the future with a voyeuring mind and a Spacial Peruser with a rewind and playback button would be able to view your most private past occasions, making them suddenly un-private. People will be surfing general space just to see if there's anything cool to watch. And what of the acquisition of dangerous, confidential, and/or security information? The possibilities threaten us as a species. Still, it would make a great app.

Question 65 & 66

Liar Liar, pants on fire
Your nose is longer than a telephone wire
                              -- An Unknown Taunter

Do you think there ever was a liar whose pants were on fire and
who had a nose longer than a telephone wire? And, in a hundred
years, when many people won't know what a telephone wire is,
will they recall the flaming fibber, or is this the beginning of the end
for this crude, whining jingle and it's legendary, blazing perjurer?

Questions 67 and 68 asked by Chicago Transit Authority. (1969)

Question 69

Why does the devil wear a cape? Is it a fashion statement? Or does his mom
make him wear it when he leaves Hell so he doesn't catch a cold on Earth?
Does the cape have any super-powers other than being flame retardant? And
the pitchfork. Do you really need a pitchfork if you're the devil? I've got to admit,
it's great branding. But is Satan planning on hand-to-hand combat and fashion
statements to cut deals for people's souls? Or to escort the unwilling to his
sweltering 'hood? I say you take away the pitchfork and the cape and what
you've got is a sweltering pantywuss. Unless the devil is for real.
Then, I'm just kidding.

Hey Look! I'm A Jerk!

How 'bout this for diversifying an existing industry: People already get buried, cremated, thrown overboard, and a bunch of other stuff when they pass on. How about getting "jerkied?"

When you pass on, you get dried out like a nice piece of meat or fruit, with a previously chosen expression, and maybe a little pepper, so your family can hang you on the wall or store you in a drawer. Or use you as drapes or a room divider. Think of all the fun on the front porch during Halloween with a hanging "jerkied" loved one and spooky glow-lights.

———

In Las Vegas, "the lesser of two Elvises" is worse than "the lesser of two evils." Calling an Elvis impersonator "The lesser of two Elvises" --well, you might as well hand him a fistful of pills and point to the bathroom.

BAUM'S FAIRY TALES

as handed down from generation to generation in my head

Smack The Lout

There was once a very old man. Well, more than once, but only once with the guy I'm talking about. No one knew how old he was, only that no one could remember him not being there. So he was either the oldest fellow around or everyone had really bad memories. Nevertheless, it was a time when, and a place where, if you were old, people thought you were wise.You grew a beard, stroked it occasionally, nodded, murmured "Hmmm" every so often, and every-one thought you were a sage. Back when being a sage meant something.

In the Dark Ages, games were often simple and often violent. The year was 892 and throughout Europe everyone was playing "Smack the Lout." It was all the rage.

Back then there were no copyrights, residuals, or royalties -- otherwise, the guy who invented "Smack The Lout," Dylan Puddler, would have made a fortune. Especially since he was famous for creating lots of games. "Tag, You're It" was his. So was "Ring Around The Rosey." If Dylan was playing it, everyone wanted to play it. Some of the then-popular games that Dylan created did not withstand the test of time -- although who really knows, because time isn't over yet. His unsuccessful efforts include: "Lick the Oaf and Make Him Cry," "No, You Kiss It," and "Hide The Fish."

One day, the very old man that I'm talking about, was playing "Smack the Lout,"
a medieval game so simple, that even the village idiot could play it. Though
when he did, he was usually the one who got smacked. At the time, our old man
was the oldest person to ever play such a strenuous game.

Our old man had just scored the winning smack, and the villagers cheered for him
wildly and for a long time. Whenever the people of the Dark Ages cheered,
they liked to cheer loud and long because when they were done cheering, they
had nothing else to do. So they loved to cheer. And boo. Man, could they boo.
After a full day of cheering and boo-ing, the Medieval spectator was bushed.

Lydia the Slavic She-Giant

Lydia stood seven feet tall and traipsed through life with a small band of nomadic pygmies living beneath her hemline. She titillated them to the extent that she, in essence, became their pied piper, and they followed her wherever she went, doing her bidding; a horny, roving family of lusting parasites and their queen. Every now and then she would summon one of them into her "Tent of Indulgence," commanding the others to play loudly outside so nothing could be heard coming from inside her nasty canvas lair.

NILES THE SNITCH

Niles the Snitch told everyone everything he was told. Especially the stuff he was asked not to tell anyone. Although, how can you say "especially" if he told every-body everything anyway. Soon, no one told him anything and he became a "know-nothing." Later, people began to use Niles to help them spread gossip, rumors, and scuttlebutt. His descendants founded TMZ.

MARTY, THE THREE-EYED CYCLOPS
(@226 A.D.)

Marty had one big eye-socket with three eyeballs in it, and was able to move each eye in a different direction at the same time. To impress girls, Marty would twitch his facial muscles up and down and roll his peepers in a circle to make it look like his cheeks were juggling his eyes. He also sported two eyelids that he could maneuver independently of each other, enabling him to play a wicked game of "Peek-a-Boo." Some thought that was cheating.

Back in Marty's day, Peek-a-Boo was very popular. They didn't have baseball, basketball, frisbee, or golf . Peek-a-boo was pretty much it. In reality, it was the predecessor of Hide-and Seek, which is basically Peek-a-boo on a larger playing field. Without Peek-a-Boo, there is no Hide-and-Seek.

Unfortunately, in the third century, Marty, The Three Eyed Cyclops was considered a freak and barely eeked out a meager living, traveling from fiefdom to fiefdom in "Crazy Murray's Travelling Marvelling Carnival." Folks would pay for a chance to beat Marty in a game of Peek-A-Boo and hopefully win a fork or a sock. In his day, Marty was the Harlem Globetrotters of "Peek-a-boo." But timing is everything. In his day, Marty was a freak. But in today's world, he would have owned a national chain of optometry shops, and wouldn't have had to marry The Duckbilled Lady.

THE ALLIGATOR AND THE WISE MAN

This is a fairy tale. That doesn't mean it isn't true. It just means there are fairies in it. At the time of this tale, there were fairies everywhere. If you sat in a garden long enough, you would probably see one go past or catch one riding a butterfly. Or vice-versa.

The last confirmed fairy sighting was in 1737, on the outskirts of Carryfurgas. Unconfirmed sightings continue to this day.

Leprechauns were notoriously fond of fairies and would go to great lengths to roo them. Some suggest there may be genetic traces of fairies in the lime-colored mulatto gnomes of Blurblebury.

By the 1700's, fairies weren't all over the place, but you'd see one every so often. Then none for awhile. Then maybe three in one day. Then none again for two weeks. Then a small bunch. Then maybe one more in three days. And two the next day. Then one or two everyday for a week. Then none for two years. Then one. And then the whole thing would start over again exactly in that order. Currently, fairies live in the imaginations of very young children and the elderly. And in those places they are very real.

And with that said ...

The Allligator and the Wise Man

They say one of the most gruesome fairy-tales ever told was
"The Alligator and the Wise Man." It was also one of the shortest. In it,
the wise man sneaks up on a menacing killer alligator, grabs the monster's
tail and prepares to flip the beast over, rub it's belly into submission, and
then finish off the behemoth with his sword, so that he may craft its' hide
into a flattering codpiece for the prince. Unfortunately for the wise man,
the alligator suddenly whipped around like a, well, like a whip, and captured
the suddenly un-wise man within it's man-slaying snout. Collectively, the
villagers realized the gator's mouth was now occupied with prey, and began
pounding the beast with oars, belts, sticks, brooms, and two purses. It was
the first wise thing they had done as a village for a very, very long time.
The moral?: "Sometimes a little wiseness, from a lot of people at the same
time, is good enough so that only one person gets eaten." You may ask:
"Where are the fairies?" They were watching from a nearby birdbath.

FAMILY JEWELS #1

This next story was recently found in my family's archives, and as far as we can authenticate, was written by Sir Leonard Baum of Fiffledown, around the transitional cusp leading The Dark Ages into the Renaissance. He was a very popular "town crier," traversing the region, acquiring and displaying the latest of everything and delivering the news from surrounding fiefdoms to each other. He told stories, jokes, performed singsongs, and tap danced. Oh how Sir Leonard could tap dance. Sir Leonard Baum was Entertainment Tonight, CNN and Comedy Central, and a PlayStation in boots. Tap boots.

By royal decree, Sir Leonard was officially declared "the unofficial emissary of the region." Sir Leonard worked Wednesday through Sunday -- much like today's comedians, firemen, and strippers. Sir Leonard Baum of Fiffledown was, and is, considered one of the preeminent story, news, and song dispersers of his day.

The following is just one of his many tales, as he told it:

QUIXLEY THE ENTERTAINER
As told by Sir Leonard Baum of Fiffledown

"Quixley, The He-She" was a very popular multi-gender contortionist, who, for anything of value, would allow you and one friend to twist and squinch him into any position -- except "The Punim-Crusher."

For years, Quixley would waddle into a town, pay a few diddles or a box of wooden yo-yos as rent for a barn or a vacant workspace, and then charge a fair price for the townsfolk to bend him "this way" and "that way" and freestyle.

Once, someone bent him too far "this way" and not enough "that way," and broke him. Every bone in his body was at least fractured. Even the inner-ear ones. Needless to say, the doctors where Quixley roamed were rotten, at best, and as a result, Quixley healed wrong. You couldn't bend him "this way" anymore. Only "that way." So for awhile he only made half as much money as he used to. It should be noted that at the time this story took place, "this way" and "that way" were two commonly known specific positions. What they looked like is pure speculation, however, as recently discovered etchings contradict each other.

What I always found more odd than Quixley's bending, stretching, and smushing, were the townsfolk that paid him to let them do it. Perhaps that's because I got to do it for free Tuesdays during warm-ups for our weekly Smack the Lout game.

Anyway, not much time had passed before Quixley discovered that because of the way his body had improperly healed, he could now juggle with parts of his body nobody had ever thought of juggling with before, thus restoring his drawing power and allowing him to once again make a very comfortable living. He became just as contortable, but in new places. Quixley developed a new act, delighting audiences as he, using only his belly and his oddly-healed nose, juggled an owl, a gopher, and a live baby, as they all fought each other. Well, the gopher and the owl fought. Poor baby.

Lyle The Cherubic Man-Maiden

Lyle could have been anything he wanted to be. He was smart, verile, and heir to his family's spoon fortune. But Lyle wanted to be a man-maiden. He wasn't effeminate or girly-like. (And I don't mean that in a negative way) He was simply a normal fellow who loved mending doilies, darning socks, and bathing people. And because he came from wealth, he could do whatever he wanted, because he didn't really have to do anything at all. His family was affluent enough to subscribe to, and live by, the philosophy: "Happy is where it's at."

I encourage you to take Lyle The Cherubic Man-Maiden, and make him a recurring character in your dreams.

Arnold and the Magic Struessle Pump

We all know the story of The Sword and the Stone, and the tales of fire-breathing dragons, frog princesses, and enchanted pigs. But just as renowned in its' day was the oft told fable of "The Magic Struedle Pump of Thistleberg. " In it, the water-pump in Thistleberg's town square suddenly, and for a while, began splashing out the most delicious apple struedel anyone had ever tasted, seemingly from the bowels of the earth. Or somewhere under the town square. Regardless, it was a miracle. Granted, an odd and somewhat meaningless one, but nevertheless, a miracle. More impressive than a burning bush, but not as flashy as parting a sea or walking on water. Still, compared to everything else that was going on at the time, it was a miracle.

By the time it had squeezed through the pump, no one could really be sure what it began as. Could've been pie to begin with. Or cobbler. And what of the spelling: struedel, struesel, struttle, streusell, streussle, struddle, struessle. Each region had it's own spelling and pronunciation. But one thing was for sure: whatever was coming out of that pump sure was tasty. Folks came from far or wide, but mostly wide, to have a taste. Back then, folks didn't mind traveling far <u>or</u> wide, but far <u>and</u> wide? Out of the question.

(CONT'D)

Frequent squirmishes pitted those who thought the pumpflow was cobbler, against those that insisted it was strudel. Bakers argued in the streets until they became so agitated they began whacking each other with their spatulas, stirring sticks, and ladles, littering the streets with broken kitchenware. But that was always good for business at Crazy Herman's Utensil Depot & Apron-arium. Locals and visitors alike would flock to Crazy Herman's for their "ladle of the week" specials. Back then a ladle was a status symbol. It was more than a spoon but less than a bowl. There were so many things you could do with a ladle: Stir, season, eat from it, in a pinch you can cook in it, measure with it, drink from it -- the list goes on. One of the prevailing axioms of the day was: "The man with a proper ladle, can eat at anyone's table."

Young Arnold of Thistleberg was the son of Morris The Baker and his wife, Claudia The Muffin Ma'am. It was while Arnold was making his daily struessel deliveries that the Miracle of Thistleburg occurred. As he passed the village water pump, Arnold stumbled, slipped, then reeled, floundered, bobbed, stumbled some more, and as he started to reel again, he slipped hard and fast, hitting his head on the spigot of the town water-pump, causing him to fall to the ground unconscious. Immediately, the pump began struedelling.

Predictably, the magic pump bolstered the economy of Thistleberg. Back then a magic strudel pump was a major thing. New inns and pubs flourished as tourism became the main industry. The villagers charged admission into town and split the proceeds. In town, artisans sold their wares, street performers performed for offerings and everyone received one free "taste" from the Authentic Thistle-burg Struedel Pump. Struedel-To-Go "from the pump" was available at Morris' adjoining bakery. He also sold an incredible likeness at a reduced price.

"What?" you may ask, ever became of Young Arnold? "What happened when he came to?" Well, Arnold remained in a coma most of his life. The first time the strudel started to get runny, someone suggested that someone else should go check on Arnold. When that someone else got there, Arnold was meandering about the room in a groggy waddle. He was promptly bomped on the head, re-instituting his state of involuntary slumber, and the pump restored the struedel to it's original consistency. Coincidence or not, superstition was very popular at the time and every time Arnold came to, someone would whack Arnold on the head until he was out cold again. Someone always kept watch.

Though since paraphrased, at the time, the moral of the story was: "Sometimes the good and welfare of the many, means a really fucked-up time for one guy."

Evil Kneebler, Daredevil Elf
(circa 1237 A.D.)

Evil Kneebler was the most daring elf of all time. Centuries before motorized vehicle jumps and jet-propelled stunts, Evil Kneebler was executing bold feats of danger like The Sponge Plunge, Giant Taunting, and Cabbage Mounting. Kneebler performed his famous stunts countrywide for royalty, fairs, celebrations, and maypole dedications.

Regretttably, Evil met his end at FairyFest, during his "Surprise the Pig" demonstration. Even as he was being sucked into the "Abyss of Slop," true to form, Evil Kneebler made funny faces and giggled "This tickles," as he slowly disappeared.

CHAPTER-IIIA

MY BAD

Shit. I'm in my office and I'm "on-hold,'" but I left the information I need on the other side of the house, and I'm calling on a hardline phone without any of the remote handheld phones in sight. And I've been "on-hold" way too long to give up my place in telephone line. I'm going to have to do a "run-and-yell."

I put the phone down, with the receiver facing the door, and bolt out of my office, through the livingroom and the kitchen -- yelling loud enough so that if an operator answers, they can hear me shouting in the distance: **"Don't hang up! Wait! I'm coming! It's me! I'm right here! I'm on the way! This isn't a machine! I'm a real person yelling! Don't hang up! I'm almost there!"** The further I get from the phone, the louder I yell. And I can't stop yelling, because if whoever answers on the other end hears any silence - boom - they're on to the next caller.

Criminey Pete, the neighbors I don't know are looking through the window from the sidewalk. They see an odd, running man yelling loudly through his house proclaiming that he's there. And that he's not a machine.

Aha! I found what I was looking for, grab it, make my turn, and head back to my office and the phone, yelling: **"Here I come! I'm almost there! Wait, it's me! I'm close. I'm reaching for the phone! Hello!?"**
It's Air Supply telling me they're All Out Of Love.

I think I sold too many tickets to the Claustrophobic's Convention. It's way to crowded. In an effort to accommodate as many people as possible, I'm diverting the overflow to Hermit-Fest. Everyone should be happy except for one pissed-off hermit. That's okay. I've already got a guy on the waiting list for next year. It's another hermit. He'll never hear about this.

Advertising circa 1142

Lars the Entrance-Maker guaranteed his work with the motto: "We stand behind our doors!" Back then that was very clever and soon led to Lars thriving as a motto-maker. "Eat at Joe's" is his. He also came up with "Oldest profession in the world." But he wrote it for a loin-cloth maker. "Stop and smell the sausage" was huge for centuries until the floral industry changed it to "Stop and smell the roses." Until roses, everyone thought sausage was the best smelling stuff around. In fact, on Valentine's Day, for years, it was not uncommon for a lady to have a romantic, touching card and a long, sweet, sausage delivered to her home or place of employment.

Larry, The Short-Tongued Lizard

A lot of lizards have two eyes that can work independent of each other. Maybe they all do. That's cool, but for me, their real superpower is their incredibly long, quick tongue that they use to catch prey -- a deadly bullwhip that at once lassos and reels in its' victim.

Unfortunately, Larry, himself a chameleon lizard, had a tongue that barely cleared his lips. As a result, he had to catch insects by hand and choke them to death. Or eat really slow things. If you're a reptile, that's as degrading as it gets.

Other chameleon lizards made jokes behind Larrys back, but whenever Larry came around, they sure changed their colors.

*****

If The Pope and a bear met in the woods, who would shit first?

My money is on the bear. After all, the Pope has already come to terms with his eternalism. The bear however, is working on instinct. And although the thought of a Pope squatting in the woods may be funny to many, in reality, the sight of a tall, bright red hat, flowing robe and a shiny, Super Bowl-like ring, could easily induce a wild bear to go poopie. It made me.

Yesterday, for the first time, I received no mail. Nothing for occupant, no ads, no current resident, nothing. Hey, I didn't get any phone calls either. Nobody had any use for me yesterday. They didn't want to sell me something, pay for anything, join a group, hangout or hookup.. For the first time, to the rest of the world, I didn't matter. My first invisible day. Man, I wish I could see those days coming. Then I could get some stuff done instead of waiting around for something to happen.

I met the man who put the "Bop" in the "Bop-she-bop-she-bop"
and he wouldn't shake my hand.

Turns out, the "man" who put the "Ram" in the "Ram-a-lam-a-ding-dong"
was actually a chick.

I know a botanist who deflowered a florist.
Hence, they're planning a nursery.

With olfactory senses way more sensitive than those of mortal men, it's...

Nostril-domous !

The man who can smell the future!

After sniffing Stephen Hawking's head and torso, Nostril-domous predicted:

Around the year 2117, a growing number of sensory-advanced "time-benders" known as The Human Cranium Rebels will have a mental breakthrough that enables them to win lottery after lottery until they own everything. Knowing that, Nostril-domous suggests that as soon as they start to appear, cozy-up to them and sign a long-term lease in a rent control district, just to be safe.

*****

It's been said that every time a bell rings, an angel gets it's wings. And they just found out that every time someone honks a horn, the devil cuts a fart.

I just saw an acid-rock-Mariachi-fusion band play "Purple Maze."

I love popcorn. But have we tried popping other stuff? Maybe there's
something better. Or just as good. Even a little worse isn't bad.
You could sell that: "Almost as good as popcorn at half the price!"

Maybe some obscure Amazon fummfle-berry tastes good popped.
If they were smarter, theater owners would try popping everything they could
get their hands on until they found a new, cheap, tasty, popping snack.
And then patent it. And make it so you can only get it at the movies.

Man, what if you had the patent on popcorn and every time someone popped
corn, you got a royalty. A little taste for a little taste.

Too bad some things were invented or discovered too soon to capitalize on
patent rights. However, a new popped thing is up for grabs.
That's where the money is. I'm going to start popping everything I can find.

THE MAN WHO SPANKED LIBERTY VALANCE

Legend has it, that before he was shot, a strange man ran in,
smacked Liberty Valance on his butt-cheeks, and then ran away.
Moments later, another guy showed up and shot Mr. Valance.

How Come? #23

You know what they don't make anymore? Sphinxes. How come? The only
recent one I know of is The Luxor Hotel and Casino in Las Vegas, Nevada.
The last good ones before that were built hundreds or thousands of years ago.
Sphinx's are great tourist attractions. They've done fantastic in Egypt and pretty
good in Mexico too.

Kansas, Wyoming, North Dakota -- these states could use a good Sphinx.
What else they got? Plus, they're easy to find because you put them in the
middle of nowhere so everyone can see it. No one gets lost going there.
How about building the first upside-down Sphinx? Now your talking tourists.
On the other hand, it's a poor use of space. Unless your selling shade.

And speaking of Las Vegas -- they replicate everything there. No need to go
traveling, it's a synopsis of the world. Paris and the Eiffel Tower, New York City
and Coney Island, Old England, Egypt, Nashville ... you name it, it's there.

Space and dimension travelers could easily mistake Las Vegas as the place
where Earthers experimented with architectural inspiration and lifestyles, and if
we liked it, we built it on a more grand scale somewhere else on the planet.
Caesar's Palace, The Golden Nugget, The Venetian were all prototypes for
Rome,The Old West, and Venice. Thank goodness for carbon dating, or we
would be hard pressed to prove otherwise to galactic visitors. And what if they
don't buy into carbon dating? How hard will we press the issue?
I say let them believe what they want.

LARRIMER'S MONARCHS

Larrimer taught his butterflies how to fly in different formations and spell out words in the sky as they migrated. He would then sell advertising to major corporations. People would see a cloud of butterflies in the sky, which was mesmerizing in itself, but then the butterflies would suddenly spell out "January White Sale At Macy's" or "CeCe's Buffet $4.95." Each generation of butterflies passed it's knowledge on, instinctually and genetically, to their progeny, so Larrimer only had to train a few hundred butterflies and he was good to go for generations.

Larrimer was constantly breeding butterflies from the original, trained flock. He toured for years at county fairs and carnivals with his word-forming butterfly act, and would challenge spectators in the audience to a spelling bee. He was very successful until he was accidentally booked with Randy's Wild Bird Show. Randy's act ate Larrimer's act, forcing Larrimer back into the mainstream of society once again. But not for long.

*****

What's with "home field advantage? Because of the fans and no travel? Right. I'll tell you home field advantage: For football, the visiting team has to play in high heels. And only the home team can wear helmets. I'll bet everyone finishes 8-8. That's a home-field advantage.

And fantasy baseball? In my fantasy baseball you get to first base, boom, you get a big kiss from an attractive woman. At second and third and home, you get a surprise pleasuring depending on how important the hit was, and so on. That's fantasy baseball.

More Grant Money Please

At the university, my experiments supported the notion that cheese is almost an animal, and that given time and ideal conditions, cheese has the potential to evolve into something that can do simple math and dress itself.

I am also very close to proving that chickens are closely related to plants. Grafting the two has been most difficult. But not impossible.

HERE'S LOOKING AT ME

I just inherited a colossal herd of gazingstock. All they do is stare at me. They won't take their eyes off me. Why me? Is there food on my face? Is my zipper down? What do they look at when I'm gone? Do they close their eyes until I come back? Do they stare at each other? Are they trying to hypnotize me? Do I hypnotize them? Are they wild when I'm gone? A well placed video camera will answer my questions. (I'll be back)

The next day:

I'm back and just viewed the video of what went on while I was gone. The gazingstock stared at the camera. The whole time. Until I got back. Then they looked at me again. Their modus-operandi baffles me. Nevertheless, they could make good money posing for art classes.

Coincidentally, the other day I'm taking a shower when I look up and see a large moth on the wall staring at me.

"You eye-ballin' me, moth?"

I don't take shit from anything. Especially a butterfly wannabe. Visually violated, I showered on. Abruptly, the moth flew headfirst into the showerhead's spray, driving it to the ground, and causing it to swirl down the drain.

Though surprised by the moth's suicidal act, somehow it was satisfying to know that other than my wife and my high school gym class, the only other living thing to ever see me naked was now dead.

*****

According to my calculations, soon, everyone will be rich from winning a reality or game show.

ABOUT LARRIMER

If you could put a scoop of Hunter Thompson, some oatmeal, and a Chinese Acrobat into a blender and hit the puree button, you might pour out a glass of Larrimer. Regrettably, because of some municipal codes, we may never know for sure.

Larrimer was raised so quickly that he was ten years old before most kids his age were five. When he was twenty, Larrimer had everything erased from his permanent record. No one knows how he did it, and he won't do it for anyone else. Distorted truths and a handmade metal ashtray from summer camp are all that remain of his youth.

Larrimer soon became a world-renowned wanderer who came home to visit every so often to regale us with a feast of exhilarating exploits. And we would boast to him of our meager adventures. But while he was in town we engaged in funstuff that enabled him to embellish stories of us wherever he wandered next.

Though most consider him a huckster-sevant, to us, he's Larrimer.

I'm watching Dr. Phil the other day and he had on this woman who had fallen into the abyss of alcoholism. She had lost her kids, her job, her family -- she was actually at the point where she was out on the streets giving men oral sex for a beer. Let me tell you something: I don't care who you are, or where you're from, that's a great deal.

Larrimer loved his privacy so much, he had one-way windows installed throughout his house. Ironically, they were accidentally installed backwards, so everyone always knew what he was up to.

What goes around comes around. But if you duck, it'll go around again.

I would never sell my soul to the devil.
However, I would consider leasing it to a gargoyle.

****

If a multi-personality hermaphrodite contortionist had group sex with itself, how would the respect be apportioned in the morning?

****

The Tupperware Party

Plastic contortions and

frilly sapped mops

turntable convenience

with storage for glops

mint condition appearance

after thousands of uses

Is there anything strong enough

to eat right through this?

I'm working on it.

PHOOEY ON DELTA AIRLINES
AND THEIR CHARITY JUICE

MINNESOTA IN JUNE
AT THE RAMADA AT THE MALL OF AMERICA

THIS IS A PERFECT EXAMPLE OF WHY I HAD TO START KEEPING
THIS DIARY AS A RELEASE FOR WHEN I'M PUT "ON HOLD" . I'VE
BEEN ON THE PHONE WAITING TO SPEAK TO A LIVE PERSON FROM
DELTA AIRLINES FOR OVER TWENTY MINUTES. FOR THE FOURTH
TIME TODAY. THAT'S EIGHTY MINUTES TOTAL. SO FAR. AND
NOTHING HAS BEEN ACCOMPLISHED. I HUNG UP AFTER TWENTY
MINUTES ONCE, AND WAS DISCONNECTED AFTER TWENTY
MINUTES TWICE. SOUND FAMILIAR? THEY'RE ALL DOING IT.
CLOGGING UP PROGRESS BY MAKING EVERYBODY WAIT.

I JUST SPOKE TO A MACHINE AND GAVE IT ALL SORTS OF
INFORMATION. AGAIN. APPARENTLY, DELTA WON'T LET YOU TALK
TO A "REAL" PERSON UNTIL YOU'VE PASSED MUSTER WITH AN
ANSWERING MACHINE -- DIVULGING THINGS I WOULDN'T TELL
MY DRY CLEANER.

CURRENTLY, DELTA HAS ME LISTENING TO A RECORDED
MESSAGE THAT IS TRYING TO SELL ME LEMONADE FOR SOME
CHARITY. DELTA AIRLINES IS ACTUALLY TRYING TO SELL ME
SOME FUND-RAISING CITRUS DRINK OVER THE PHONE WHILE
THEY PISS ME OFF OVER THE PRODUCT I CALLED FOR -- THEIR
CORE PRODUCT: AIRLINE TICKETS. BAD IDEA. FIRE OR DEMOTE
THE PERSON WHO GREENLIGHTED THAT IDEA. BESIDES, I HAVE
BASIC RULES THAT I LIVE BY. AND ONE OF THEM IS:
NEVER BUY LEMONADE FROM AN AIRLINE COMPANY.

(cont'd)

PHOOEY ON DELTA AIRLINES AND THEIR CHARITY JUICE

SO, DELTA WANTS TO SELL ME LEMONADE BEFORE THEY SELL ME AN AIRLINE TICKET. NO WONDER THEY'RE LOSING MONEY. WHERE ELSE DO THEY DO THAT? YOU EVER CALL FOR AN INSURANCE QUOTE AND BEFORE YOU TALK RATES THEY PUT YOU ON WITH A FIG SALESMAN? YOU EVER CALL A RESTAURANT FOR DINNER RESERVATIONS AND THEY TRY TO SELL YOU A CHARITY LUBE JOB? NO. IT DOESN'T HAPPEN.

AND SHAME ON YOU DELTA. YOU ARE PUTTING PRE-SCHOOLERS AND FIRST-GRADERS OUT OF WORK. YOU ARE TAKING VITAL BUSINESS LESSONS AND OPPORTUNITIES AWAY FROM CHILDREN WHOSE ONLY SALES LOCATION IS THEIR CORNER, AND THEIR ONLY PRODUCT IS LEMONADE.

HOW MANY NEIGHBORHOOD LEMONADE STAND CLOSINGS WILL IT TAKE FOR YOU TO BACK OFF? WHAT'S NEXT? YOU GONNA MOW LAWNS AND DELIVER THE NEWSPAPER TOO? HOW ABOUT YOU LEARN HOW TO ANSWER THE FRIGGIN' PHONE AND SELL AIRLINE TICKETS? GET ME MY FLIGHT, THEN MAYBE I'LL TALK LEMONADE. BUT PROBABLY NOT. HOW 'BOUT THIS: I'LL JUST GIVE THE MONEY TO YOUR CHARITY. FORGET THE LEMONADE. I GOT MY OWN PEOPLE FOR LEMONADE. NOW IF YOU OFFER ME SOME BUTTER-SCOTCH TWEETLES OR A NANA-KRUMBLE, I'M IN. OR A RAFFLE TICKET. I CAN CARRY THOSE AROUND IN MY POCKET. OR SAVE IT FOR LATER IN MY BRIEFCASE. I CAN'T DO THAT WITH LEMONADE. AND HOW ARE YOU GOING TO GET IT TO ME? YOU GONNA MAIL ME LEMONADE? DON'T YOU DARE TELL ME IT'S POWDERED LEMONADE. THAT'S NOT LEMONADE. THAT'S A PIXIE-STICK WITHOUT THE STICK.

PHOOEY ON DELTA AIRLINES AND THEIR CHARITY JUICE

AND IF I DID BUY YOUR CHARITY LEMONADE, HOW DO I KNOW MY
LEMONADE CHARITY MONEY WILL GET TO WHERE IT'S SUPPOSED
TO GO? YOU DON'T HAVE ENOUGH PEOPLE TO ANSWER THE
PHONE, LET ALONE SOMEONE TO GET THE LEMONADE MONEY
OVER TO YOUR CHARITY. BY THE WAY, DO YOU KNOW HOW MANY
TIMES I'VE BEGUN OR FINISHED A BUSINESS TRANSACTION WITH
A LEMONADE PURCHASE? NEVER. AND I'M A PUSHOVER WHEN IT
COMES TO LEMONADE.

I JUST BRIEFLY SPOKE TO A DELTA AGENT AND SHE DIDN'T HAVE
ANY OF THE INFORMATION I TOLD THE MACHINE. SO I ASKED HER:
"WHAT HAPPENED TO ALL THAT INFORMATION THAT I JUST GAVE
THE MACHINE? WHERE DID IT GO? AND MY VOICE? NOW YOU HAVE
MY VOICE STORED SOMEWHERE TOO!? IN TODAY'S CLIMATE OF
IDENTITY THEFT, YOU COULD SELL MY VOICE AND MY INFORMATION
TO SOMEONE WITH NEFARIOUS INTENT, AND THEY COULD
MANIPULATE THAT INFORMATION IN A DASTARDLY WAY. A
COMPANY COULD CAJOLE A CORRUPTABLE IMPERSONATOR TO
STUDY AND IMITATE MY VOICE, OR HAVE AN AUDIO TECHNICIAN
DUPLICATE, MANIPULATE, AND/OR EDIT MY VOICE TO CREATE
CONVERSATIONS I NEVER REALLY HAD, WITH PEOPLE I DON'T
KNOW, IN AN EFFORT TO FRAME ME OR WREAK IDENTITY-THEFT
HAVOC ON ME. OR YOU. YOU'RE BEING RECORDED TOO. HOW
MANY IMPERSONATORS AND AUDIO TECHNICIANS WILL NOW GO
TO THE DARK SIDE? KEEP YOUR EYES ON THEM."

SHE MUMBLED AND WENT TO FIND OUT WHERE MY VOICE
AND INFO WENT. SHE'LL NEVER BE BACK. AND SHE'LL NEVER
FIND OUT THE ANSWER. NOT THE REAL ONE ANYWAY.

(cont'd)

A BUNCH OF MINUTES LATTER

UNBELIEVABLE!   DELTA STILL HAS ME ON HOLD!

IT COMES DOWN TO "RESPECT." RESPECT FOR THE CALLER'S
TIME. THIS IS WHAT HAPPENS WHEN COMPANIES EXPAND
FASTER THAN THEIR ABILITY TO POPULATE THEIR BUSINESS
WITH COMPETENT EMPLOYEES. OR THEY FIRE THE COMPETENT
ONES FOR CHEAPER, INCOMPETENT ONES. IN THE FUTURE,
UNLESS I WANT TO PURCHASE LEMONADE BY PHONE AND HAVE
IT MAILED TO ME, I WILL AVOID CALLING DELTA AIRLINES .
IT'S A WASTE OF PRODUCTIVITY FOR EVERYONE INVOLVED.

I CAN'T BELIEVE DELTA AIRLINES WENT THROUGH ALL THE
TROUBLE OF BUYING SOMES AIRPLANES, PAYING AIRPORTS
TO LET THEM LAND AND TAKE OFF, ADVERTISING, HIRING PILOTS,
CABIN CREWS, MECHANICS, BAGGAGE HANDLERS, COUNTER
PEOPLE, LAWYERS, ACCOUNTANTS, AND YOU LOSE ME WHEN I
COME TO BUY YOUR PRODUCT. AT THE POINT OF SALE.
I WANT IT -- BUT YOU MAKE IT TOO HARD TO BUY. YOU ACTUALLY
GOT ME TO YOUR "STORE" READY TO BUY, AND THEN TREAT ME
POORLY **AND** TRY TO SELL ME LEMONADE.

"EFFICIENCY" AND "COMPETENCY" IS THE ANSWER TO MOST
OF DELTA'S PROBLEMS. "CANDY" IS THE ANSWER TO THE REST.

FORGET ABOUT THE LEMONADE, IT'S OUT OF YOUR LEAGUE.
SHUT DOWN YOUR VIRTUAL JUICE STAND AND CONCENTRATE
ON SERVICING ME. I WANT TO BE SERVICED . I'LL EVEN PAY
EXTRA TO BE SERVICED. I DEMAND SERVICING!

NEVER MIND. I'VE DECIDED TO WALK.

.

YOU NAME THIS CHAPTER

Can you name a recent Miss America? Exactly. What we need is a good ol'
trash-talking Miss America. A babe with "Muhammad Ali mouth." Someone
so talented and so beautiful that she could rag on the other contestants, insult
the judges, talk dirty, maybe flash the crowd, and still win. The Terrel Owens
of pageantry, if you will. I know I will. A Miss America who spikes her victory
bouquet, then taunts the runner-up, proclaiming, "That's right! That's right !"
That's a Miss America we can market. You'll remember <u>her</u> name.

****

Earlier today someone told me, "Tomorrow is the first day of the rest of your
life." That would make today the last day of the first part of my life. I wish I had
known a little sooner. If I had known that today was the last day of any part of
my life, I would have planned a party. Maybe a roast. But I'm not sure I want
to start another part of my life tomorrow. First off, I'm not ready, and second,
I'm kind of on a roll.

And if I ever get caught in that sliver of time where the first part of my life ends,
and the rest of my life begins, can my "now" get squished?

STRIPPERS, WANNA MAKE SOME MONEY?

Here's a free marketing idea for any strip club that needs a free marketing idea: Put this sign in front of your business:

LAP DANCE SPECIALS!

"Freebird"	**$15**
"In-a-Gadda-Da- Vida" **(w/drum solo)**	**$20**
"Bolero"	**$25**
"A Hundred Bottles Of Beer On The Wall"	**$60**
(or $25 per 30 bottles)	

What If

As long as I can remember, which changes daily, I've wondered how different my life would have been had I been born a caballero. No doubt I would have bigger hats. Anything else is a guess.

2:30 am -- July 29
(I am "on hold" with the shitty,expensive,shitty ,wireless, shitty, internet provider at the hotel regarding their shitty, expensive, intermittent service. Other than that, the hotel is great)

I'll tell you what has really slid in popularity: Turnips. No one talks about them. No one orders them in restaurants. Nobody brags about their turnip fortune. When was the last time you heard someone say, "Hey, do I taste turnips in this?"

There was a time when turnip money had juice. Not now. Squash and cilantro money have passed turnips. Until recently, cilantro was big here and there and nowhere else. Now, it's global. Even the Swedes use it to season their ice-pies and blubber cakes.

In competitive Rhumba circles, Larrimer is known as "The Loopy Dervish."
Whoever said "It takes two to Tango", obviously never saw Larrimer dance.
Not long ago, in Latin America, a petty spat over why Larrimer shimmies and
how he shakes turned into a medium-sized war between two tiny countries.
Since then, one of those countries was absorbed in a corporate merger and
other quit and became a full-service resort. And that is where I am right now --
vacationing at The Pleasure Island Resort, relaxing at the Hickory-Daquiri-Dock,
a marina-side, umbrella-drink bar, run by an ex-clockmaker and his mousy wife.
The rides here are all in your head, but they're pretty cool. Yesterday, I went on
The Joe Cocker Rock n' Roll Rodeo Ride. I saddled up on a mechanical Joe
Cocker and tried to ride him for 8 seconds while he sang "Hitchcock Railway."
It certainly was different, if not fun.

Everyone on the island is talking about how this year's hurricanes have skirted
by their island because of the "crystal harmonizer" that a local new-age-ist
erected to protect The Pleasure Island Resort with "synchronized eco-vibes
from deep inside the universe's soul."

The next day The Pleasure Island Resort took a direct hit from Hurricane Paul.
And when I say a direct hit, I mean the hurricane actually formed right over the
harmonizer "protectorant." Crushed the fuck out of it. Like it was a hurricane
magnet. Then it sucked up what was left like it was hurricane food.
True story.

****

SHAME ON YOU MY CABLE COMPANY
SHAME SHAME SHAME

STOP THE MADNESS WHILE YOU CAN

For crying out loud, who's saving money when I have to talk to four different people from four different countries, to correct My Cable Company's mistake -- causing me to spend an hour of my day up to this point talking to people who don't understand me and vice-versa. Because it's cheaper FOR THEM? Not in the long run. Eventually, with this kind of service, they won't have anybody left to service. The only thing My Cable Company has ever done consistently is be unreliable.

To resolve My Cable Company's latest error, I first talked with a woman in Manilla. I explained to Ms. Manilla that I had paid my cable bill through My Cable Company's automated phone system and that my credit card company had recorded my cable bill as "paid," but My Cable Company hasn't credited it . Ms. Manilla and I would have understood each other better if we were mooing.

Because we couldn't communicate, I asked to speak to someone in The United States. So I was transferred to a guy in India. I'm guessing that's what she thought I asked for. That, or she was fucking with me. I asked the guy in India if I could speak to a supervisor who didn't have a supervisor. He said he was bad at math and transferred me to a woman in Mexico, who was a "supervisor-in-training." Oh, so close.

(cont'd)

Now, I'm sure these are all nice people, but we're wasting time.
A good percentage of callers must just give-up. Of course.
That's why they do it. It's their "Labyrinth of Defeat." Callers feel
"F-it" and move on.

From now on, when anyone calls me, I'm going to tell them:
"I am Baboosh, Mr. Baum's client services representative in
Spitsbergen. Would you like to leave a message?"
After that I will just mumble.

Wait! I think I got transferred to the U.S. -- Gotta go -----

MOMENTS LATER:

Nope. Talked to someone briefly, but I'm "on hold" again.
Ticked off.   Three deep breaths... relax... must ... try...to write...

***

OBSCURE HISTORY

From 482 until 894, the most popular event in the forests of
Bavaria was PillageFest. Most references to it, except for the
Plunder Ball, were purged from history during the Renaissance.
The main problem was, it took a week to plan, and a year to clean
up after. By the time everyone finished cleaning up from the last
PillageFest, it was time for another one. It ended when everybody
decided not to clean up anymore and just moved away.

****

MY CABLE COMPANY CALL -- CONTINUED

Can you believe this isn't over? I'm back "on hold" AGAIN with My Cable Company. It's later in the day. I've gone out and done stuff, come back, and still...

Earlier today I eventually spoke to someone who claimed to be in the U.S. I explained that my credit card company is reporting that MY CABLE COMPANY has been paid, but My Cable Company doesn't have it credited. He asked me to call my credit card company, get the authorization number and call back with that information. I did that, so now I'm "on hold" waiting to give some-one the authorization number.

Something about The Olympics is on in the background.
It's about fencing. Fencing should be called "stabbing."
If it was called stabbing, more people would watch.

***

Human on the line. Got to go.

MOMENTS LATER

I gave a new guy the authorization number, he checked and told me they still don't have any record of the transaction, and if I would call the credit card company back and....

(cont'd)

"Stop right there," I said. "You guys have me playing telephone ping-pong and you're the hole in the net. Everybody else did what they were supposed to do. Except you. YOU find out where the sludge is in your cyber-pipeline. YOU call my credit card company - here's the number - YOU call them and resolve it."
He agrees.

LATER THAT SAME DAY...
CAN YOU BELIEVE IT? OH, THE HORROR OF IT ALL

I went about my day and when I got home there's a message from my credit card company, left by a real human, on my answering machine, letting me know that My Cable Company called them and that My Cable Company assured my credit card company that they had corrected everything and that my payment had been credited. Oh joy.

I decided to check anyway. Maybe I'm anal. Well, not maybe. But I've learned during my "war against incompetence" that assurances are no assurance. If they've fucked up once, they can, and usually do, fuck up again. And again. A leak in the hose doesn't fix itself. So I call the automated system and -- Bingo! -- no change to my account. I press 0 and wait once again to speak with a cable company representative. In cave-man days My Cable Company people would already be dead, unable to survive primal Neanderthal tempers.

(cont'd)

Got a rep on the phone. I got a new guy and explained everything, and he began: "Oh, I see here it says we talked to your credit card company and everything... wait a minute, let me talk to my supervisor." And he's gone. I would have said, "No. Let ME talk to your supervisor," but I never got the chance. "On-hold" isn't even a choice. You're just tossed there.

He returns with: "My mistake. We haven't talked to anyone yet."

"Really you fuzz-fuck?" is what I wanted to say. What I did say was, "I just happen to have a voice message on my answering machine from my credit card company that verifies you spoke to them earlier and you assured them that you corrected your error. Here, I'll play it for you."

I held the phone next to the speaker of my answering machine, and we both hear:

"Hello Mr. Baum this is Michael from Your Credit Card services department, and we just wanted to let you know we spoke with Your Cable Company and we verified your payment and they assured us that they have corrected the problem and credited your account."

After a moment of silence I begin: "Didn't talk to anyone? It's on your fucking computer screen. You started to read it to me. Would you like to go ask your asshead weasel-lipped supervisor what you should do now?"

"I'll credit your account right away, Mr. Baum."

"Great. And right after you do that, cancel my cable and internet account. I'm going satellite!

****

Baum's Fairy-less Tales

As told by future tellers in hindsight

No Fairies Tales

No one remembers why the humans left Earth, or if they really did. But upon their return centuries later, humans, following directions found on an orbiting satellite, discovered three identical history books entitled "Tales From Planet Earth" hidden on our planet in secret locations. "Tales From Planet Earth" was a chronical of events that were considered momentous, and essential knowledge for any Returner.

One of the books was found hidden at a Himalayan mountaintop monestary. Another was retrieved from a remote underground Amazon cave. The third was in Elton John's garage.

How do we know these tales to be true? Because of the accuracy regarding the events we do know about, their credibility regarding those we know nothing of, has become unquestioned.

The following tales are portions of what was found.

OLD MAN KRUGER'S BOY

Call it mutation, evolution, creationism or coincidence. Whatever it was, Paul Kruger, circa 2058, was the first in a series of humans born with the gift of flight. It was both amazing and unimpressive, because Paul could only fly about a foot off the ground. At about three miles per hour. So he couldn't really save anyone, but he could distract someone who was breaking the law until help arrived. Sometimes. That was helpful now and again, but he never became a bona-fide hero.

What should have been an evolutionary landmark, actually looked silly. "Fliers" in the beginning had problems. Some could fly real high, but couldn't get down, and we had to slingshot them their food and supplies until they could be retrieved by rescuers with jet-packs. Others could fly very fast, parallel to the ground, but couldn't control themselves, causing some funny, yet tragic accidents that became very popular viral videos.

BOOTY AND THE FEAST

The Epicurean Years

The year was 2548, and humans were no longer at the top of the food chain. Nor were they smartest living thing on their home planet. It was the Epicurean Era. The Epicureans had voracious, yet gourmet appetites and carried most of their weight in one of their many rear-ends. Behind their backs we would call them "Medussa-ass." But never to their faces. To stay alive, the people of Earth became an army of phenomenal chefs. It was a matter of survival. As a species, we were considered the best cooks for galaxies, if not the universe. During this time, our survival depended on our culinary talents.

When the Epicureans first arrived, they loved the taste of our ears. Our ears were considered "the truffle of the Milky Way." An Epicurean would approach a human, stand on his or her feet so they couldn't run away, and then rip off their ears and eat them. They did it so fast, it almost didn't hurt -- like pulling a bandage off of a boo-boo real fast. And that's all they wanted. They didn't want to kill you, or eat anything else of you. As a matter of fact, it was not uncommon for an Epicurean to pull off your ears, eat them right in front of you, and then ask if you wanted to go grab a beer. They ate the ears of other animals too, but apparently ours "were to die for."

Earthers learned to make everything else taste so delicious, that it was seldom necessary to eat human ears. And, for the most part, most of the recipes for humans were bogus and intentionally meant to make us taste rancid. If the Epicureans ever caught on, they played dumb. Because of our willingness to please, Epicureans were fond of saying: "A good human is an Epicurean's best friend."

Why they suddenly left is still a mystery. Some suspect they had reservations somewhere else.

THE HARMONY ORDINANCES

The Harmony Ordinances were left by the Grammartarians -- a peaceful, perfectionist civilization so advanced, they redefined simplicity. And many other words too. They were strong, honest and wise, but aggravatingly obsessive-compulsive about correcting mistakes. Some planets like that. More about them soon.

The only difference among all the tales found in the three separate cylinders, was in the Harmony Ordinances. All three documents contained The Ordinances, but in different orders. There are two schools of thought: One, the order matters, and two, the order doesn't matter. For a while, the ones who thought it didn't matter splintered into groups that fought over how much it didn't matter. Regardless, after the Grammartarians visited, virtually the entire globe lived in relative peace by honoring the following ordinances:

THE HARMONY ORDINANCES

1. CLEAN UP YOUR OWN MESS.
It doesn't matter if it's ketchup drippings on the side of the bottle or
a sloppy camel utter -- you clean up your own mess.

2. TAKE A SHOWER AT LEAST ONCE A DAY.
This Code had a dramatic affect on the world, as irrigation systems
had to be built to enable everyone, everywhere, to shower.
Showers were even set up in remote outposts in case someone
on Earth got really lost. The planet became healthier, cleaner, and
society advanced faster than ever before because there were less days
of productivity lost to illness or disease and everyone felt fresh and zesty.

3. NO BITING. AND DON'T KILL ANYONE EITHER.

4. WHEN YOU PROMISE SOMETHING, YOU DO IT.

5. TIP <u>AT LEAST</u> 15%.

6. LEAVE EVERYONE ALONE UNLESS THEY GIVE YOU PERMISSION TO DO WHATEVER IT IS YOU WANT TO DO TO THEM. THEN, EVERYONE TRY TO ENJOY IT.

7. NO BULLSHIT. AND IF YOU HAVE TO ASK, IT'S BULLSHIT.

THE GRAMMARTARIANS

The Grammartarians loved to correct spelling and grammatical errors.
They thrived on it. It was the center of their existence. They spent their
time on Earth as they did on other planets: correcting all the spelling and
grammar errors throughout history. In books, movies, brochures, tests,
mail, and journals. You name it, if it needed correcting, they wanted to do it.
They had a separate spaceship just to carry their red correcting pens.
It was like video games to them. It was their thing. They'd come to your
planet, correct all the spelling and grammar errors and leave. To be honest,
they were quite good at it. They went through and corrected every-thing in
two months. Even the hieroglyphics. Then they took a short nap and left.

*****

One wave of aliens came to Earth in peace, loved our planet, but had
extremely sensitive ears. They couldn't tolerate the noise from leaf blowers.
Drove them crazy. They could hear them from continents away and it made
them extremely agitated. The aliens gave us three months to come up with
a quiet leaf-blower. We thought they'd be flexible and tried to negotiate a
fifty-percent noise reduction within ten years.

By ignoring their ultimatum, they were so offended by our arrogance, they
began launching Earthlings into space in barrel-sized space pods. We got
the point, and soon the planet was nice and quiet. Perhaps that's how we
got to Earth in the first place -- By pissing something off on another planet
and getting blasted here.

How Come #91

There was one piece of Earth-logic most "space visitors" had trouble with.
It was the "two negatives make a positive" rule. "Why then?" they would argue,
"don't two positives make a negative?" The yin here is missing its' yang.
Apparently, our planet is the only one where the double-negative rule applies.
Everywhere else, two negatives are still a negative. And a super-negative at that.

****

THE DIMENSION WARRIORS

A small band of Dimension Warriors passed through in the twenty-fourth century.
They were mighty and ruthless, but they had paws instead of feet, and that
proved to be their Achilles heel.

One night, we covered the entire planet with lubricants and banana
peels, then attacked. In battle, The Dimension Warriors flailed about comically
like a dog running in place on slick linoleum. As they were slipping, sliding, and
giggling, we picked them off like ducks on a pond, winning our first slapstick war.

****

The Looky-Loo People came to Earth just to watch our wet T-shirt contests.
When we stopped having them, they left.
Then we started having them again.

CHAPTER 37

WHERE'D THEY GO ?

It's hard to find a good tinker. Sometimes things don't need a full repair, they only need a little tinkering. But nobody tinkers anymore. If there was just one good tinker in town, I'd wager he'd have to train new tinkers to help with his tinkering overload. You can't even find a decent tinker teacher. And I've tried. It all has to be self-taught, with none of the secrets usually handed down by a tinkermaster.

I am told that in Europe, in small villages nestled away from any hub-bub, plying the trade of their ancestors, are the last tinkers.

Where did all the tinkers go? Many became what we now know as the much more expensive "handyman."

Uncle Sandy, laying on the ground, yanked me by my ankles and whispered wildly from the floor: "I am Eighty-Five! And never before have I appreciated the soft touch of a young woman's naked flesh against me as much as I do right now. And never before has that reality been so remote." Then he placed a small doll's dress over my left shoe and took it to the movies. I got the shoe back from Uncle Sandy weeks latter, and it was the first time I ever saw a shoe look humiliated.

***

Forget about the mouth, is it okay to look a gift horse in the ass?
If not, where can I look a gift horse. Is the ear safe? How particular
are they? I have a feeling there's nothing wrong with looking a gift horse
in the mouth. There's worse places you could look. I mean, what good
is a gift horse if you can't look it over?

As far as anyone knows, Larrimer is the first hydroponically-raised human. His parents were locally renowned philosophical botanical-nutritionists. They perished during a hypothetical drought. Larrimer never consumes solid food, per se. He inhales prepared, nutritionally enhanced vapor, steam, or mist from a special bank of foggers. For a snack, he'll breathe the wild minerals, vitamins, and other essentials present in his immediate airspace. I have seen him sniff a room sterile. I have seen him inhale someone's aura and burp out a libido haze. I've seen Larrimer do things that only his doctor and his gardener should know about.

***

So here's my question: When a light bulb is burned out or missing from a light socket and the power switch is flipped to the "on" position, is there electricity trying to get out from there? And am I being charged for it? I mean, does the electricity, the switch, and the lamp socket know the bulb is gone or burned out and that there's no light in the room? And do they notify the meter? Or do I need to get a lightbulb in there real quick?

Getting Grandpa Home

Grandpa had a German Shepherd dog named Thunder fastened to his belt with a long leash. Thunder was trained to get Grandpa home before sundown, because at sundown, Grandpa feel asleep. No matter where he was or what he was doing, at sundown Grandpa was "out cold." Like a dyslexic bat. So, if they were out past sundown, Thunder would drag Grandpa home, through the front door, to his bedside, and leave him resting on a previously prepared comforter on the floor.

When he first got Thunder, Grandpa would wake up startled after being dragged just a few feet, grumbling in discomfort. It happened often enough though, that key parts of Grandpa's body got callous and the tow home became numb, and confortable, so Gramps got his sleep and arrived home safely.

*****

Yesterday I heard someone yell: "Get Help!" It was either that or "Get Whelped." To be safe, I did both.

Young King Phinapus

At the ripe old age of four, young Phinapus was crowned King.
No pressure here. Even if kinging were his calling, at four it's tough
to rise to the occasion and properly mete out justice, champion social programs,
behead people, war, and preside over public floggings, assorted ceremonies,
as well as food and sex orgies. Until coronation, Phinapus' biggest credit was
that he no longer needed a bib. A week ago he was still crapping in his pants.

And if you <u>are</u> good at it at four years old, you're washed up by eleven.
How do you impress anyone? Everyone starts complaining, "sure he's twelve,
but you should of seen him at four. The country's infrastructure was refurbished,
taxes went down, everyone had healthcare and a diploma. Back in the day,
man could that boy rule. Now? He's coasting on his laurels." Or it was:
"Of course he's a good king. What do expect, he's twelve. He's been kinging
since he was four."

You can't top a good four-year-old king.   Wait!
How about a coronation at birth?

Attila Re-visited

Attila the Hun called his army The Hunnies.
That would make the enemy laugh and give Attila's soldiers
an upper hand during an attack. It's hard to fight hard when
you're laughing. It sacrifices the integrity of your animosity.
It's almost impossible to win a war while you're laughing.
Almost.

*****

If a man and a woman with multiple personality disorder had all
their personalities performing sex with each other at the same time,
would that constitute an orgy? Could a climax be enjoyed
individually by each personality, in effect producing a mind reality
of simultaneous, multiple orgasms, by a number of people,
converging in overlapping currents, channeled by a group of
personalities into just two persons shivering with streaming,
industrial strength pleasure?

Excuse me, I have to towel off.

Larrimer and the Adage

Larrimer never bought into the adage "You don't know what you've got until you lose it." He firmly believed "You never know what you've got until you've got way too much of it." He reasoned if you had way too much, you could always get rid of some of what you got until you knew what you had.

***

Perhaps the greatest salesman of all time is the guy who sold the world on pimento-stuffed olives. He actually talked the olive people into pitting their product, then stuffing it with something else right into the place you just wanted something removed from. With something nobody really needs. I'd rather have the pit. Plus, I've never met a pimento farmer or met anyone that knew a pimento farmer. Or anyone talk about their "pimento money." And what are pimentos made from? Is it a plant or is it an animal? What the hell are we eating?!

***

I just taught my nose how to play with my ears while I'm sleeping. That way, when I'm awake, they're too tired to do anything but smell and listen. Another problem solved.

THE HOMESTRETCH

I was watching Dr. Oz the other day, and he said that for every thirty pounds a man loses, his penis grows an inch. I figure if I can get myself down to about sixty pounds, I'll look like a centipede dragging a troll.

I have created a new shape. I've shown it to seven people, but only four could see it. I have found that those who can't see my new shape get very upset when they're around others who are admiring one. And the ones that <u>can</u> see it are very arrogant and tease the ones who <u>can't</u>. Curse the day I discovered the flebtangle.

I just spent the entire day writing analogies.
Do you have any idea what that's like?

UPGRADE TIME

Time-out for an upgrade. For rat poison. It kills rats. It also kills people.
And cows. And corn. And ducks. And anything else that consumes it.
Every once in a while you hear about some woman who has killed her
husband by putting rat poison in his food. Or vice-versa. And that's "cut"
rat poison. Mixed with food. Which means even diluted, it will kill a man.
Recently, someone's cow got into some rat poison and it killed the bovine.
In India, a circus elephant licked a rat that had just eaten rat poison and the
elephant died. Not really, but the other stuff is true. I think. Regardless, rat
poison kills everything. Hence, it should be officially reclassified as: Poison.
Forget about "Rat". Yes, it kills rats, but that's about the smallest thing it kills.

It is both humiliating and degrading for a large animal to be slain by a poison
made to eradicate something smaller than its' foot. Rat poison should be
safe for dogs. It's not. But no one's going to buy Dog Poison. And if they
do, arrest them. In truth, rat poison should only make humans feel woozy.
At worst, a person should maybe get a little rash, a little fever, maybe the
runs. It starts here. And it starts now. What is now known as "rat poison" is
now officially: "poison." Live your life from this moment on thusly. It should
inspire someone to develop something that only kills rats. They could grab
the vacant "Rat Poison" moniker and have it all to themself.
That's where the money is.

TRUE STORY

A confused man once said, " Once a comic, always a comic."
No one was sure what he meant, but allow me to construe:

A pure comic performs for no one. And anyone. The pure comic
performs for the cosmos -- realizing that what *is* funny, *is* funny,
regardless of any response. The universe knows. It doesn't matter
if there's an audience or if anybody "gets" it. All that matters is that
in the scheme of things it is funny. The true joke need not be coddled
by audience approval. It was under such a Sartre-like presumption
that the following took place:

Although years ago I told a bastardized version of this true story in my act,
I have transcribed it more faithfully, with names and places, while "on hold,"
at the request of others.

In reflection, I'm not sure if it was the early 1980's or late1970's, but they
were almost identical anyway. Except for disco. Besides, the '80's get a
lot of credit for what happened in the '70's. Same with the '60's. They get
kudos for stuff that really happened in the '70's. Regardless...

I was performing at The Comedy Store in San Diego with Garry Shandling and Jeff DeHart. Jeff went on first and then disappeared. At the end of the night, after looking all over for Jeff, Garry and I headed back to the car and found Jeff asleep in the driver's seat, his head resting on the steering wheel. Most folks, upon seeing their buddy in this condition would gently wake him and offer to take over the driving duties for the ride home. Most folks would. Garry and I looked at each other and then instinctively, without a word, Shandling, giggling ever so softly, the way he does, opened the front door and slid into the passenger seat. With Garry set, I heaved myself onto the hood of the car as Garry whacked Jeff on the shoulder yelling: "Look out!!!" just as I landed with a big thud on the hood of the car. Jeff, thrust from a deep sleep into a seemingly instant life-and-death situation as he opened his eyes, screamed "Oh No!" as he frantically spun the steering wheel from left to right as he tried not to hit anyone else with his motionless car.

If Jeff didn't soil himself, it sure smelled like he did. The stinky car made us laugh harder. And gag. Which made us laugh even harder. By the time we stopped laughing, we were home.

True story.

MORE FAMILY ARCHIVES

Also found among my family archives were a number of poems
by a Milton Baum of Bohemia. He wrote avant-garde poems
during the 1800's. All of his poems began:

Namby pamby porcelain shoes
Cracked underfoot just to amuse
Bumblesnouts and whiffle-greens
sweet and pert and still unseen

After that, the poems got weird.

The Cousteaus Should Know

Has a whale ever tried to mate with a submarine? And, if so,
were the sailors in the sub entitled to a smoke afterwards?
Or is that something no one ever talks about again.

I used to live near **"Abbey's Sick Room and Party Supply."**
I always wondered: "Who's gonna kill two birds with one stone
in that store?" Anyone ever going to walk up to the counter
going over their shopping list and say, "Let's see, I'm gonna need
a colostomy bag, a bedpan, two intravenous stands, and...
oh yeah, some confetti and two of those Whoopee piñatas."

When are you going to use all that stuff at the same time?
I guess anytime you plan on having over a group of carefree
incontinents to bludgeon a farting, candy-filled, hanging doll,
it's time for a visit to Abbey's Sick Room and Party Supply.

I KNOW WHY

Shouldn't we be working on unleashing the potential of the brain
so we can control the dispersal and re-assembling of our
body mass, enabling us to climb aboard a light source and travel
at the speed of light, re-constituting at a new location anywhere
along the path of the light source. You know why we don't?
It would destroy the transportation industry as we know it.

Larrimer stood up, and in a stream-of-consciousness blurted:
"I believe mirrors retain images as well as reflect them!" Suddenly, a large
dictionary fell off the shelf above, onto Larrimer's head. Larrimer paused,
stumbled for a moment, waddled some, then skipped around the room,
singing:

A puddle of chocolate
drifts in my navel
as chili fries eye it
from across the table

A hat made of noodles
a mitten of crow
socks made of lime rhine
underpants of dough.

Larrimer abruptly stopped and sheepishly tip-toed out the front door,
acting like we couldn't see him, as we all quietly waved good-bye.

I'm Good With That

Grammatically speaking, quotation marks have a lot of balls.
What audacity. They demand to be "all encompassing."
None of the other punctuation signs make you do that.
Even the question mark and exclamation thingy show up
in the middle of a sentence as an expletive replacement
once in awhile. But quotation marks have to come before
and after everything. Or else it's marked wrong. Why?
Even if I want to end with a period, like this: "Hello".
No, I have to go: "Hello."   What if I want the period to be
all-inclusive, to change the lilt and subliminal respect via
punctuation control of the sentence? Screw grammar.
If you understand me and I understand you, I'm good with that.

I just found Godot. He says he couldn't find his keys and he's sorry everyone had to wait. Now I'm off to find Guffman.

As the mimes yelled for help, the silence was deafening.

I try to look at snoring as nose jazz. It makes me more tolerant.

For Siamese Twins, does it take three to tango ?

Back in the day, the pre-fix "town" before your occupation had cachet. It was a real compliment if you were the "town" something. Every town had a "town barber," a "town crier" a "town doctor," and so on. If you were the "town" something, everyone knew who you were. If you were just "a blacksmith," you probably weren't great at what you did, or new at it, and a lot of people had no idea who you were. But if you were "the town blacksmith," then you were something. When folks referred to "the town blacksmith" everybody knew who they were talking about.
As long as you weren't the town idiot, drunk, or whore, the "town" label could only help. If you were the town idiot, it was tough to get work. No one wanted to say, "Yep, the job is done. I had the town idiot fix it."

Also, none of the nice ladies in the county wanted to boast, "The town idiot is my boyfriend!" On the other hand, the few times the town idiot was a woman, she had lots of dates.

How Come ? #7

Last night I was preparing to cook a frozen pizza in the oven. The directions said to preheat the oven to 450 degrees for ten minutes. Why do I have to let it be 450 degrees for ten minutes? 450 degrees is 450 degrees. Does the pizza know how long it's been 450 degrees? Does time make it MORE 450 degrees? Are there degrees of 450 degrees? How 450 degrees can you get?   As far as the pizza is concerned, it's 450 degrees right now and that's all that should matter.

The moment the oven hit 450 degrees, I told the pizza it had been like that for an hour and shoved it in.

The Masseuse-opus

If we're talkin' inter-species genetic breeding, then let's consider breeding a masseuse with an octopus. Eight arms and eight hands that can massage four people at a time, averages about $300 per hour plus tips, and pays taxes. It's a win-win for everyone.

Some Answers

This is legal? Now they have recorded messages calling my house to put me "on hold." From the Philippines. And India. I pick up the phone and it's: "Please hold for an important message." Yeah? From who? Tell me who's calling, you shit. Don't hide overseas. Come ring my doorbell and then hide. Then I'd have a chance to catch your ass and use my spankpaddle again, restraining order be damned. Fuck you. Next time you call, I will wait for a person and I will audio-bludgeon their ears with an amped bullhorn into the receiver. This has gone too far.

What kind of homeland security is it when everyone at a call center in Mumbai has access to your identity. You think it's tough to nab an identity thief here in the United States? Try catching Pissysing Snurpee who's living large in Jakarta as Bruce Baum. Who's idea was it to "spread the identity?" I'm sure it wasn't a woman. They should glue his balls to the bottom of his feet and make him run a marathon. On hot sand. That should deter that kind of thinking.

***

I'm "on hold" with the pool repair place. I've got to make sure there wasn't some kind of mistake. I just had my pool heater repaired. Took less than an hour. The parts were only $28.75. However, I just paid $178 per hour for labor to have my pool heater fixed. A hundred and seventy-eight bucks per hour for labor for a pool heater repair? That's as much as a mediocre lawyer or a shitty surgeon makes. More than a pharmacist. And a teacher. Combined. Times two. That's where we should start. The epicenter of adjustment is clear. We start at jacuzzi repairman gets $178 per hour and everyone else's salary is adjusted from there.

Anybody got a problem with that?

TAG! That last chapter was "it."

I feel much better now. Now you try.

EXTRA-LOGUE

EXTRA-LOGUE
Not part of "ON HOLD."

I would like to make it very clear that the book "On Hold" has
ended.It's over. What follows is not part of the book.If you like it,
feel free to leave it in. If you don't like it, feel just as free to
rip it out, and you still have a complete copy of "ON HOLD."

Most of those in the small cadre of folks I had read my
ramblings during my On Hold Experiment said to leave this
stuff out -- that it wasn't good enough for the book. So,
I, unlike me, listened to others and left them out. So they are
not in "ON HOLD."

However, when I went to publish my book, I found there are
increments of pages you must order and it's not necessarily
the number you want. This meant I was going to have a few
blank pages at the end of ON HOLD.

Aha! The bar had been relocated. Not lowered, but relocated.
Now, itstead of having to be good enough to get in the book,
this stuff only had to be better than blank pages. So I asked
myself: Are the next few pages better than nothing?
I thought they were. But you judge. If not, I apologize.
Again, if you don't like it, rip it out, and you still have a complete
book. You can always let me know what you think by e-mailing
me at: Bruce@BruceBaum.com

BETTER THAN NOTHING ?

Age Discrimination

When you're two years old, and when you're about eighty years old,
you can run around naked in public and it's accepted as cute, or at least
tolerable. But try that shit when you're thirty, and they lock your ass up.

***

I've been organizing Hermit-Fest. So far there's two guys coming --
a plumber, and a guy who's not a plumber. And I'm afraid if they find out
about each other, *they* won't come.

The Plumber found out about the guy who is not a plumber and cancelled.
Who could of told him?

***

If two Jews walked into a bar and no one was there, would it still be funny?

***

Nobody runs like Larrimer. In fact, no one has ever been able to describe
the way Larrimer runs. It has to be seen. Normally, if someone gets close
to describing it, they pass out.

(Title after poem)

Potatoes Au Gratin
Hold the cheese
chili fries
And hold the beans
What you say
Ain't what you want
Welcome to Kaleidoscope Restaurant

Take a prism
and grease the edges
feed the dog
if he squirts the hedges
Tuck your shirt
Into someone else's pants
Then let yourself do
The Kaleidoscope Dance.

Bouncy bouncy bouncy
On your neat nerfy ass
Laughing and flirting
Like a schoolboy on the first day of class
We both say "my bad"
And hold back a sneeze
and ask, "May I dance with you slowly
Through Kaleidoscope Scenes?"

Close your eyes
And squint your face
inside-out to please the place
Lube your medulla
with Aurora Borealis schemes
Welcome to Kaleidoscope Dreams.
I'll Just Have A Root Beer

Last night I dreamt the movie "Diana Ross and the 3 Stooges."
It had everything you could want: Diana Ross nipple-twisting Moe,
head-slapping Larry, and giving juicy woo-woo kisses to Curly.

I just ate an entire upside-down cake backwards.

You know what a vacation is? You pay someone to make sure
nothing happens to your place, while you go fuck-up someone else's.

I just got asked to leave The Santa Barbara Zoo. Apparently I put
the laughing hyenas and the mockingbirds too close to the paranoid animals.

You can always find out what Bruce is up to at:

BruceBaum.com

Coming Soon or Already Out:

"The Adventures of BabyMan" comic book

Other books by Bruce Baum

Letters From A Nut   co-authored as Ted L. Nancy

More Letters From   co-authored as Ted L. Nancy

Extra Nutty   co-authored as Ted L. Nancy

(Even More Letters From A Nut)

Made in the USA
Columbia, SC
01 July 2022

62586253R00067